D1530002

GETTING A JOB IN
THE FOOD
INDUSTRY

RITA LORRAINE HUBBARD

ROSEN
PUBLISHING®

NEW YORK

Thanks to Thomas and Marcus Hubbard, Markeyda Haywood, and my friend Ellen Fike for sharing their food service stories. Special thanks to my editor Bethany Bryan—who has the patience of Job—and to my mentor, W. C. Hunter, for his steadfast friendship and decades of tireless instruction.

Published in 2014 by The Rosen Publishing Group, Inc.
29 East 21st Street, New York, NY 10010

First Edition

Library of Congress Cataloging-in-Publication Data

Hubbard, Rita L.
Getting a job in the food industry/by Rita Lorraine Hubbard.—1st ed.—
New York: Rosen, c2014
        p. cm.—(Job basics: getting the job you need)
Includes bibliographical references and index.
ISBN 978-1-4488-9606-6
1. Food service_Vocational guidance—Juvenile literature. 2. Food industry and trade—Vocational guidance—Juvenile literature. I. Title.
TX911.3.V62.H83 2014
647.95'02—H8612

Manufactured in the United States of America

CPSIA Compliance Information: Batch #S13YA: For further information, contact Rosen Publishing, New York, New York, at 1-800-237-9932.

CONTENTS

INTRODUCTION

So you want to work in the food industry. You've decided that college isn't for you—at least not right now—and you want to explore your job options. Congratulations: you've just made the first of many important decisions that will come your way as an adult.

But what is the food industry, anyway? Is it just bussing tables and stocking shelves, or is there more to it?

To answer your question, the food industry is a large group of companies, organizations, institutions, and individuals that grow, harvest, process, ship, market, and/or cook food. They eat it, too, but that's another story. Food industry jobs range from selling hot dogs from a food cart on a busy street corner to preparing gourmet meals on an ocean cruise ship. But before we explore the jobs, let's look at the experience of one teenager working in the food industry.

Markeyda was sixteen when she landed a minimum wage summer job as a cashier and prep cook at Church's Chicken. She had zero experience, but she was a hard worker with a good attitude and a flexible schedule, and that's exactly what the employer was looking for. Each morning, she set her alarm clock to ring well before 6 AM so she could get to the restaurant before 7 AM. It was extremely important for her not to be late because her

Food service jobs like this one are demanding by nature. This waitress has been on her feet for hours but still sees that each customer's food arrives at the table hot and on time.

job included counting out a certain number of chicken legs, breasts, wings, and thighs and placing them on long cooking trays to refrigerate until the fry cook was ready for them. If Markeyda was late, the chicken pieces wouldn't be ready, and if the chicken pieces weren't ready, the fry cook would be thrown off schedule. If the fry cook was thrown off schedule, the entire restaurant would also be thrown off schedule and unprepared when the rush-hour crowd arrived.

Markeyda's job also included mixing biscuit batter and scooping out two hundred biscuits each batch, then refrigerating them until it was time to bake them. She also "dropped" fries and corn and scooped mashed potatoes and other sides into family-sized or single-sized cups. These were placed in the food warmer for later.

Her job involved lots of standing, mentally and physically calculating payments, and dealing with unsatisfied customers. Her advice to other teens is, "Be prepared to use your mind. Know how to add and subtract without the cash register. Learn the menu and prices so you can work faster and more efficiently, because when you have to hunt for prices, you slow the process down."

Jobs in the Food Industry

Now that you have an idea of what a typical day in the food industry is like, it's time to take a closer look at the wide range of jobs in the industry. Remember, food covers lots of industries, but we've narrowed it into three distinct fields for you here.

Food Service

Restaurants, hotels, caterers, and fast-food restaurants are always in need of cooks, bakers, food handlers/prep cooks, servers, and hosts/hostesses.

Cooks and Bakers

Cooks are usually responsible for seasoning and preparing dishes like soups, gravies, and vegetables. If you decide to become a cook, you will have several positions to choose from. As an entry-level prep cook, you would probably arrive long before the other restaurant workers and stay to clean up long after they are gone. Even though the word "cook" would be a part of your title, you would probably do little or no actual cooking; rather, your job would be to chop or peel certain foods, measure seasonings, and prepare the cooking area for the head cook's use. You might also wash dishes, take

Restaurant kitchens are usually fast paced and intense. As second in command to the executive chef, this sous chef is working hard to serve a dish that is both delicious and pleasing to the eye.

out the trash, store unused food or ingredients for later use, and operate special kitchen appliances to grind, chop, and/or mix ingredients. This type of kitchen experience provides excellent on-the-job training (OJT) and is a great way to work your way up to becoming an actual cook.

If you are hired as a short-order cook, you will learn to prepare quick and easy dishes that take a short amount of time to cook and serve. These dishes might include chili dogs, cheeseburgers, cheese toast, or pizzas; in short, any dishes that can usually be prepared quickly on a hot grill. This is the reason short-order cooks are sometimes called grill cooks.

If you become a line cook, you might cook specialty foods like burgers or omelets, but you would not be responsible for overseeing the entire kitchen. You would work under a head chef or head cook, and your responsibility would be whatever dish or whatever area of the kitchen he or she designates. For example, your area might be the grill only, or you might be solely

TEN STEPS TO STARTING YOUR OWN PRODUCE STAND

1. Make sure your location is easy to find and easy to get to by car or by foot.

2. Reach out to local growers, do a close-up inspection of their produce, then discuss prices and quantities. Don't make a deal until you know for sure you'll be able to open your business.

3. Go to your local city government before you spend any money and find out the rules, regulations, and permits involved with opening a produce stand.

4. Ask friends and family for suggestions. Depending upon the season you open for business, you'll need to know which fruits and vegetables are in high demand. Avoid stocking items that are unpopular or out of season.

5. Tune up your truck. You're going to need a reliable way to transport large quantities of fruits and vegetables from the growers' gardens to your produce stand. No transportation, no business.

6. Set up your stand. Make sure your place is neat, clean, and safe.

7. Wash your fruit. You'll need access to water to clean off your produce before you sell.

8. Check your cooler. Fruits and vegetables won't last long if they're not kept cool. Be sure you have a way to keep your produce from wilting or spoiling because you may not sell everything in one day.

9. Count your money. Make sure you keep enough change in your cash drawer to make change for your customers.

10. Have fun.

responsible for making cold sandwiches or dishing up the salads. You would probably work alone in your area of the kitchen, but it is not unheard of for line cooks to supervise other kitchen assistants.

If you become a baker/pastry chef, you will make delicious pastries, pies, breads, and desserts. In some restaurants, a baker's job is different from a pastry chef's job. The baker would make all of the above bread products, and a pastry chef would make cakes and pastries only, but no bread. As a baker-in-training, you would start your entry-level job as a baker's assistant and would probably shadow the head baker/pastry chef to learn how to measure and mix your ingredients, bake or fry the batter or dough, and produce good-smelling, eye-pleasing pastries for the customer. With experience, you could become the executive baker, and in that capacity, you would supervise the other bakers, designate which desserts should go on the menu, and be responsible for the kitchen inventory.

Hard work, dedication, and hands-on experience as a prep, line cook, or baker's assistant could lead to your becoming head chef, head baker, executive baker, or even kitchen manager.

Servers and Hosts/Hostesses

If you are hired as a server, your job will be to seat customers, take orders, answer questions, serve food, and take payments. Although some servers may make this job look laid-back and easy, that's just not true. Servers have to be masters of multitasking. They must take care of several tables at once, with each table capable of holding several customers. They must answer

Servers need stamina and dexterity to be able to remember orders, balance food plates, trudge back and forth from the kitchen to the dining room, and answer questions—often all at the same time.

questions, remember orders, time food so that they bring it out steaming hot at the right time, work with the bartender, restock tables, and return to tables they have already served in case the customers still need anything.

While it may seem that a host's or hostess's only job is to stand at the door and greet people, this is a misconception. Hosts or hostesses work just as hard as servers. If you became a host or hostess, you would greet customers as they enter, answer questions about the specials for of the evening, arrange for seating, take telephone reservations, and check on orders.

All of these jobs start at minimum wage (or just above) and require long hours on your feet, either in the dining area or in a hot and busy kitchen. There may also be extra duties attached to these jobs, like packaging and storing leftover food, taking out the trash, washing dishes, wiping tables, answering questions, and cleaning the work area. You would probably have to pass a drug screening and background check, but the good news is that you probably wouldn't need prior experience; OJT (on-the-job training) is usually enough. There's also room for advancement. With a few years of experience as a hostess, you could become a supervisor or floor manager.

Working in a Cafeteria

Working in a cafeteria is a little different from working in a restaurant. Cafeterias do need cooks, bakers, food handlers, and dishwashers, but they don't always have a table staff. This means customers will either visit the steam tables themselves or will form a buffet line and make their selections as they walk past the servers.

Hospitals, schools, nursing homes, corporate dining areas, and department stores all have cafeterias. If you choose to work in a department store, you will probably be needed only an hour or so before and after the lunch hour, and the menu will probably be limited to sandwiches, hot dogs, and fountain drinks. If you choose to work in corporate dining, you may be

Although cafeterias typically have no kitchen staff, they can still be as busy as regular restaurants. Here, customers form a line and walk past serving trays to choose their dishes.

needed for luncheons and dinners, and the dining area would probably have a fancier setting for VIPs, including covered tables, dinnerware, and table service.

Since hospitals, schools, nursing homes, and military bases serve breakfast and lunch, and all of these (except schools) serve dinner, your work hours would be longer and more intense if you worked in one of these settings. You would be serving hundreds—and in the case of schools and military bases, perhaps thousands—so you would need to report very early in the morning to help prep huge amounts of food, fire up the grills, set up the condiment trays, and stock the money drawer to make change. You might have to keep a running inventory of food and supplies or file invoices and receipts.

Since you would be an entry-level employee in each of these cafeteria settings, you'd most likely earn minimum wage. Many of these jobs require a background check, physical examination, and possibly a drug screening. Also, remember you'd be working in a hot, crowded kitchen and would have to deal with all sorts of personalities, so you would need to be extremely flexible, get along well with others, and have a pleasant and easy-going personality. With hard work, dedication, and practice, you could advance to shift manager, kitchen manager, or assistant cook.

Product Handler

Long before the food is ready to be cooked, it must be processed by product handlers. As a product handler, you could work in the warehouse of a big corporate food service company, such as Kraft, Campbell Soup, or General Mills, where you might stack boxes, take inventory, operate machinery, or be a delivery driver. In addition to a high school diploma or GED, you would need to pass a physical examination, a background check, and a drug screening. You would also likely need a special driver's license.

Working in Grocery Stores

If you decide to work in a store rather than at a corporate food service company, you have many jobs to choose from. As stock boy/girl at a grocery store, you would meet delivery trucks at the cargo bay, lift and unload boxes, store extra boxes of food or supplies until needed, and stack individual

This stock person takes extra care to make the shelves look neat. By placing products closer to the front, the shelves not only have a fuller appearance, they are now easier for customers to reach.

items on store shelves in an appealing way so customers can find what they need.

If you choose to become a butcher, your work would be very detailed and would require lots of OJT (on-the-job training) under an experienced butcher. You would learn to receive, inspect, and properly store all types of meat for freshness and quality, and you would keep records of how much meat you issue to certain cooks or restaurants per day or week. You would learn to safely use machinery to slice, weigh, trim, bone, and grind beef, pork, poultry, or fish in a way that makes it mouth-watering and irresistible to customers. You would also be asked to cut special orders for customers. You might be asked to explain how to best bake, fry, or broil certain meats, and you would be the one to decide when meat should be placed on sale before its expiration date.

As a deli worker, you would learn to safely slice, weigh, and wrap different meats, cheeses, vegetables, salads, and sandwiches. You might season, prepare, and cook delicious rotisserie chickens, arrange eye-pleasing condiment trays, hand out meat or cheese samples, and even tell customers about different products and services being offered in the deli.

Farming

Although farming is listed last, it's definitely not the least important of the three fields. In fact, it's

These farmer's assistants are feeding and watering healthy pigs that will eventually be used for human consumption. Animals require special care to ensure they are safe for eating.

probably the most important, since vegetables, grains, and meats all come from farms and ranches.

Did you know there are plenty of jobs to choose from in the farming industry? Crop farmers (horticulturists) need help growing and harvesting fruits, grains, herbs, nuts, vegetables, and even sugar cane. They choose (or even harvest) the best seeds, then plant and maintain them. This maintenance includes pruning, fertilizing, cultivating, harvesting, and storing their crops until it is time to sell them. And of course, selling them includes packaging, pricing, and marketing their crops.

A livestock farmer raises and breeds animals that are sold to other farmers or are used for food. Livestock farmers may raise cattle, chickens, sheep, pigs, or goats. Whatever they decide to raise, all of their animals must be fed, housed, and cared for to remain healthy and disease-free so that they can be sold for human consumption. For these reasons, livestock farmers can always use a handy assistant.

Aquaculture farmers raise fish like catfish and trout for resale and work long, irregular hours at varying shifts to make sure the water quality is correct, the fish are healthy and well fed, and breeding conditions are right. Like other farmers, they can always use a young assistant who is ready and willing to work, but it must be mentioned that the aquaculture profession is a slow-growing industry, and jobs are sometimes rare.

As a farmer's assistant you would assist the farmer with whatever needs to be done on the farm. You might operate farm machinery to till, fertilize, weed, and water certain areas of ground where the crops are grown, or you might use your hands to plant seeds and pull weeds. If you find work at a fish farm, you might feed the fish, remove dead fish, check the water quality, and look after the equipment. If you work at a livestock farm, you might feed and water the animals, clean stalls, put out fresh hay, or feed the chickens. This means you might need to be outside in all kinds of weather, doing all types of physical work for hours at a time.

If you are hired as a seed harvester, you would learn to harvest and process seeds for resale to other farmers, which includes boxing, stacking, transporting, and mailing packages that are up for sale. If you train as a mushroom grower, you would learn to plant, fertilize, grow, and harvest mushrooms for local or regional buyers. This would include processing the mushrooms, storing them for transport, and delivering them to buyers.

Produce Stands

You might also consider working as a produce stand assistant, or you could become a business owner and start your own produce stand. As a produce stand assistant, you might be responsible for contacting local growers, purchasing their crop, and delivering it to the produce stand. Or, you might receive the boxes of produce off a delivery truck, then unload and arrange the produce so that the customers can see and get to it. You might also water flowers, spritz fruit, operate the cash register, answer questions, and carry customer purchases to the cars.

Whatever position you choose in the farming and produce industry, you'll need a pleasant personality, the ability to follow directions, and lots of energy to withstand the

This woman works at a produce stand located on a private farm. She spends much of her day arranging and restocking produce baskets so customers can easily find what they need.

hard work and heavy lifting that goes along with jobs like these. Formal training is probably unnecessary, but you would probably be expected to catch on quickly when you are offered on-the-job training. You would likely need to pass a background check and/or a drug screening and a physical examination. Most of these jobs begin at minimum wage or slightly above, and all of them would probably require you to have a flexible schedule in case an emergency arises.

What You Need to Know Before Seeking a Job

Now that you know what types of food jobs are out there, it's time to think about job hunting. Of course, there are a few things you should know before you begin looking for a job, like how to represent yourself well. One way to do this is to craft an impressive résumé and cover letter. This section will help you do that.

The Résumé

A résumé is a document that presents your background and experience at a glance. Résumés have seven basic sections: contact information, objectives, education, work experience, skills, honors and awards, and references. Following is a breakdown of each section.

The contact information section is located at the top of the first page and is the first thing your prospective employer will see when you give him or her your résumé. This section includes your full name, complete address (even if it's only temporary), city, state, and ZIP code. It should also include your home telephone number, cell phone number, and e-mail

Your résumé will often be an employer's first impression of you. Be sure it is neat and clean, and represents your professionalism well. Have a friend go over it to ensure it is error free.

address so the employer can easily reach you if he or she decides to call you in for an interview or offer you a job. Make sure your telephone and cell phone voice messages are professional.

The objectives section is where you'll write a short statement about what you hope to do, learn, experience, or become. For example, you might write, "My objective is to gain experience as a chef by working closely with experienced chefs who will teach me how to season and prepare different meats and soups."

The education section gives employers an overview of where you went to school, your course of study (although most high schools follow the same course), and whether you received a diploma or a GED. You will type the name of your school; the city, state, and ZIP code; the telephone number, the last grade you completed, and your GPA (grade point average) if it is higher than average.

The work experience section may be the skimpiest section on your résumé because as a student, you may not have that much experience in the work world. Just remember to list every type of work you've ever been paid for. That includes babysitting, dishwashing, housecleaning, or even washing a neighbor's windows or cutting his or her grass. In other words, if you were paid to do it, list it.

The skills section is where you'll list all the things you know how to do. For example, you might know sign language or speak a second language. You might be Internet-savvy, or you might know how to build Web sites. Whatever your particular specialty, you'll write about it here.

In the honors and awards section, list any honor roll awards, honorable mentions, dean's list, club ribbons, or listing in "Who's Who Among High School Students." If you were commended for perfect attendance, lettered in a sport, or were nominated for homecoming queen or king, list these honors, too.

In the reference section, you'll be expected to identify people who know you, know your work ethic, and can vouch for your character. Many applicants choose to write "References available upon request" in this section, and then they produce the references on the date of the actual interview. Whether you include the reference details on the résumé or on the day of the interview, be prepared to list the names of at least three people who know you well and who are not your relatives.

Make sure you get permission to use each of your references' names so that the follow-up telephone calls they receive from the employers won't come as a surprise to them. There is nothing worse than listing the name of a person you haven't spoken to in years because the odds are that the person won't know what to say if an employer calls.

Include each reference's name, home and cell phone number, address, and city, state, and ZIP code. Tell how long you've known each person and in what capacity you know him or her (e.g., classmate, friend, teacher, or pastor).

Writing a Great Cover Letter

After you complete your résumé, you'll need a great cover letter to go with it. The cover letter should be at least three paragraphs long and should explain all the things your résumé can't. For instance, in a cover letter, you could discuss how long you've admired the business, what good things you've heard about it, and what a good fit you feel you'll be for the workplace.

You'll introduce yourself in the first paragraph by writing something like, "Good afternoon. My name is James, I'm a

Take advantage of your guidance or career counselor's expertise and get help constructing your résumé and cover letter. While you're at it, ask for a written recommendation.

native of Chattanooga, and I'm very interested in working for your company." Feel free to use this introduction in your own cover letter, but remember to tailor it so that your own personality comes through. In other words, be yourself and talk about your own situation.

In the second paragraph, you'll talk about your skills and experiences. For example, you might write, "I've never had an official job, but I cut grass for my parents and my neighbors. I also earned money raking and bagging leaves." If you have any technical skills, you'll want to be sure the employer knows about them. You could write, "I taught myself how to build Web sites, and now I manage a blog online, where I chat about the latest video games." Whatever you decide to write, remember that this is the place to toot your own horn to get the employer's attention.

In the third paragraph, mention how the job will benefit you. You might write something like: "I've always loved to cook, and

If the school's computer lab is off limits after school hours, you can always use the public library's computers to search out information about local businesses and job openings.

grew up helping my mother in the kitchen. I love making desserts, and I feel that getting this job as a pastry assistant will help me learn some important techniques I can use later as I work my way to becoming a head baker."

There are many resources that can help you write a great cover letter, so take advantage of what you can find in your local library, on the Internet, and in your guidance counselor's or career counselor's office. It's fine to compose a generic cover letter that you can use again and again, but when you find a company that is hiring, be sure to address the cover letter to a specific person. Most people don't like receiving letters that begin with "Dear Sir or Madam" because this seems very cold and impersonal, as if you don't care who reads the letter.

Do a little research to find out whom you'll be working for or who'll be doing the hiring, and address the letter to that person. This makes the letter more personal, which in turn makes it more memorable to the employer. He or she will appreciate that you've made an extra effort to find out his or her name and will feel that you are serious about making a good impression. One way to find the person's name is to make a few phone calls to the receptionist or assistant of each business and ask to whom you should direct the letter. If he or she tells you just to put "Dear Sir," explain that you want to make your letter personal, and you would really like to know who supervises the position or manages the business.

Once the receptionist or assistant gives you the name, be sure to check the spelling of it. You may be an excellent speller, but even if the person has a simple name like "Steven Smith," ask that the receptionist spell it for you. "Stephen" could very well be spelled "Steven" or "Stefan," and "Smith" may be spelled "Smithe" or "Smyth." So as you craft your letter to "Mr. Stefan Smyth," tell him all about yourself, your goals, your skills, and your hours of availability. And after you have done all this, don't forget the most important part of the letter: don't forget to ask for an interview.

Using the Three Ps in Your Job Search

As you prepare for the big job search, remember that three of the important aspects of job-seeking all begin with the letter P. We call them the Three Ps: politeness, preparedness, and persistence.

The word "politeness" means to have a sense of courtesy and respectfulness toward other people. Job competition is extremely stiff these days, and unemployment is a huge problem. Don't be surprised if, in addition to competing with other young people, you're also competing with adults, even retirees, for the same job. Employers may work long and hard during the day but still have to conduct dozens of interviews to find the right person to fill the position. They will probably ask the same questions and listen to the same answers dozens of times before they make a final decision. With that in mind, politeness is an absolute must because it's a sure bet that a poor

You may have to submit dozens of applications before you find the right job, but no matter how long it takes, keep a pleasant attitude. A smiling face goes a long way.

attitude—or a fantastic one—will stick out in a prospective employer's mind.

The word "preparedness" means to be in a state of readiness at all times, in case an opportunity you've been waiting for finally opens up. There's nothing like being prepared, because when you are prepared, you increase your chances of achieving the goal you have set for yourself. But preparedness doesn't just mean having your résumé and cover letter neatly typed and ready to distribute at a moment's notice, although that's certainly a good thing. It also means thinking through all the details about yourself and your situation, from beginning to end.

For example, you'll want to be sure you have a reliable way for employers to reach you, so you should make sure you have a valid e-mail address and a cell phone that is not in danger of being deactivated for any reason. You should make sure your landline has voice mail (or is at least hooked up to

WHAT EXACTLY IS A BACKGROUND CHECK?

A background check is an investigation in which an employer gathers information about you that you may not have volunteered to tell in an interview. Background checks have been known to uncover all sorts of things, including negative driving records, school absenteeism, criminal activity, fake Social Security numbers, fake references, previous employment that ended badly, and fake diplomas. But just to be clear, employers aren't necessarily trying to find bad things about you; they just want to make sure that what they find won't make a difference in your job performance or pose a risk to other employees.

an answering machine) in case you miss the call. You'll also want to have reliable transportation, but if you don't have a car, you'll want to know the bus schedule like the back of your hand. You'll also want to be sure you have as flexible a work schedule as possible. But beyond all these things, you'll want to have perfected a back-up plan, just in case any of the ways in which you've prepared yourself happen to fall through.

In summary, you'll want to practice preparedness by thinking ahead and doing all you can to make it easy for an employer to hire you.

The word "persistence" means being determined to stick to your course of action, despite any difficulties or

In today's job market, people from high school to retirement age may apply for the same job. For this reason, applicants will need to find a way to stand out among the competition.

obstacles you may face, and regardless of how things look at the time. As mentioned, today's job market is extremely competitive. Many once stable jobs have completely disappeared due to the struggling economy, and new jobs are not being created as quickly as citizens would like them to be. This means that dozens, maybe hundreds of people are all competing for the same jobs, and unfortunately, many of these people will lose out. This news can be disheartening, but don't panic; just remember, persistence is the key. It would be wonderful to get a callback after the very first application you submit, but that rarely happens. In the real world, you may have to submit dozens of applications, online and in person, before you get a callback. Be prepared for a "no" or two, and don't take any of it personally. Just keep pounding the pavement, searching the newspapers, and turning in applications until you find the job for you.

CHAPTER THREE

The Job Search

Now that you've finished your résumé and cover letter, it's time to begin the job search. But first, take this quick quiz to see if you're really ready for work.

"What?" you may be thinking, "I'm almost out of school and I need money now. Of course I'm ready."

Well…not necessarily. You see, people who really want to work exhibit certain characteristics, so you should make sure you have those characteristics before you commit to any job.

Work-Readiness Checklist

Answer the following fifteen questions truthfully. Remember, if you answer dishonestly, you'll only be hurting yourself. If you answer "no" or "sometimes" to any question, that is the area you need to tweak. When you finish, look over your answers and jot down things you might do (like setting your alarm clock an hour earlier so you can get used to rising earlier) or changes you might make (like paying special attention to directions and details) to improve your work-readiness skills. Afterward, show your checklist results to a parent, guidance or career counselor, or someone you know with work experience and ask him or her to give you tips and suggestions on how to work on your employability and work-readiness skills.

It's never too early to improve your work-readiness skills. Get into the habit of rising an hour or two earlier now so that you're used to it when you do finally land a job.

1. You find it easy to wake up early and get going in the morning.

    ( ) Yes ( ) No ( ) Sometimes

2. You're very dependable.

    ( ) Yes ( ) No ( ) Sometimes

3. You're usually on time to class or scheduled appointments.

    ( ) Yes ( ) No ( ) Sometimes

4. You have a pretty good idea of the types of food industry jobs that would be a good fit for you.

    ( ) Yes ( ) No

5. You have neat, clean, typed copies of your résumé and cover letter to give to each prospective employer you meet.
    ( ) Yes ( ) No

6. You have an interview outfit that is appropriate for the job you're applying for.
    ( ) Yes ( ) No

7. You get along well with others.
    ( ) Yes ( ) No ( ) Sometimes

8. You don't mind being told what to do.
    ( ) Yes ( ) No ( ) Sometimes

9. You follow directions well.
    ( ) Yes ( ) No ( ) Sometimes

10. You have reliable transportation.
    ( ) Yes ( ) No ( ) Sometimes

11. You have at least three references, with addresses, phone numbers, and e-mail addresses, who have given permission for you to use their names on your application.
    ( ) Yes ( ) No

12. You have an e-mail account with an appropriate username.
    ( ) Yes ( ) No

13. You have an active landline and/or cell phone, and each voice mail is professional.
    ( ) Yes ( ) No

14. You're prepared for the questions a prospective employer might ask you and have practiced your answers so you know what you're going to say.
    ( ) Yes ( ) No

15. You've prepared a list of questions to ask the employer, such as how often you'll be paid or if there's room for advancement in the company.
    ( ) Yes ( ) No

Finding Job Leads

Now that the prescreening checklist is out of the way and you have a good idea about your own skills and work readiness, begin your job search by making an appointment with your school guidance counselor or career counselor. Your counselor's job, among other things, is to help young people develop a career plan, so he or she should already be aware of any upcoming job fairs and job openings in the community. your counselor may offer group or individual résumé-writing sessions, so be sure to sign up for a session if one is available. Also, he or she may even be willing to write a letter of reference for you, so don't be shy—ask.

Once you've met with a guidance counselor or career counselor, check in for status updates from time to time, but by all means, don't stop there. The Internet is a great place to conduct a job search, so take a pen and a pad with plenty of clean paper for taking notes, and head to the library or your school's computer lab. Run an Internet search to find out if your local newspaper posts classified ads on its Web site. Conduct your search by choosing your favorite search engine (e.g., Google or Yahoo!) and typing in a search phrase like "Chattanooga News Free Press Classified Ads." You may also search for your city's department of employment security to see what jobs are listed there. For instance, you might run a search for "Hamilton County Department of Employment Security" (substitute your county's name), then see what this search yields. Jot down (or print, if possible) all the jobs that seem as if they would be a good fit for you.

If you don't have access to the Internet, you can always do things the old-fashioned way and pick up a newspaper to read

Get to know your guidance or career counselor well because his or her office is the place to learn about job fairs, job seminars, and other activities that may lead to employment.

the classified ads section. Some guidance offices subscribe to the local newspaper, so check there first. If there is no available copy, you can always stop at a grocery store, newspaper vending machine, or gas station and purchase a paper. Read each ad carefully and jot down the jobs that seem to be a good fit for you.

Be sure to keep detailed notes about the jobs you intend to apply for, including job titles, locations, the date the ad was placed, and so forth. These details will help you keep your job search organized and will help you avoid applying for the same job twice, which has been known to happen. Make a habit of reading each ad twice, so that you understand what the employer is looking for. Follow each ad's directions to the letter, because one of your first tests may be to see whether you follow the directions that have been laid out in the ad. If you ignore those directions, you may in fact be showing the employer that you don't understand what is being asked of you and leading him or her to believe that you'll behave the same way in the workplace.

Job Fairs

Job fairs are recruiting events that bring businesses and job seekers together under one roof. They can offer great opportunities for finding a job or a career, and they can also be very exciting, because there are few other instances in which job

Job fairs can be wonderful opportunities to show employers what you're made of. Come prepared to wow the employers at the job fair by first practicing your interview skills at home.

seekers will have such access to so many different businesses, organizations, and employers at the same time.

As a job seeker, you should learn all you can about the job fair before you attend. Many fairs will post the list of companies and employers on the attendance roster, and you should be able to learn about this list from your guidance counselor or career counselor. This will give you a heads-up about what each company does, what types of openings they have, and how each company may be a good fit for you. This is also a good time to practice your interview skills, so do plenty of role-playing with a friend or family member, where your friend pretends to be the employer and asks questions about your job experience. This way, you'll know what you're going to say when you meet a job fair employer face-to-face, and this may help the interview go more smoothly.

UNUSUAL JOBS IN THE FOOD INDUSTRY

As you know by now, the food industry isn't just cooking, washing dishes, or seating customers. There are all types of jobs in this industry, and some are very unusual. For example, did you know you could become an ice cream tester? A chocolatier? A chewing gum chewer? You could even be a food writer, like the woman in the movie *Julie and Julia*. There is a new "back to vegetable gardening" trend that's sweeping the nation, and most of these gardening organizations maintain gardening blogs that could always use a great blogger. In this case, you could be a gardening blogger who blogs about when to plant, how to harvest, how to can your own vegetables, and even different ways to cook them.

Employment Agencies

If none of these job-seeking methods yield good results, you might consider using an employment agency to help you find a job. Employment agencies advertise jobs online and in the newspapers just like regular employers, but they are not the ones doing the hiring. They simply represent employers who are looking for competent employees.

You should know that employment agencies may charge a fee for their services, but many times, the company that is doing the hiring agrees to pay the fee for you. Whether or not there is a fee, the good thing about using an employment agency is that companies in need of workers keep the agency posted about open positions, and the agency, in turn, keeps you posted.

Agency staff will ask you to come in, complete an application, submit your résumé, and have a face-to-face interview with one of the agents. Since the agency is very familiar with the company doing the hiring, the agent may help you tweak your résumé so that it stands out even more, coach you about your answers, and give you tips about how to dress and make a good impression. You may even receive certain job training skills before the agency sends you on an interview with a prospective employer.

Other Ways to Search

While you are making use of all these methods, you can also use another tried-and-true method of job hunting in your search. It's called "keeping your eyes open." You see, not every business advertises its job openings in newspapers or on the Internet. Some business owners prefer to simply hang signs in their windows. So, as you ride the bus to and from school, walk to the corner grocery, or ride in the car with your family, keep your eyes peeled for "Now Hiring" or "Help Wanted" signs in store windows or stand-alone lawn markers.

Tip: If you see a "Now Hiring" sign in a store window, and if you're dressed for an impromptu interview, take the opportunity to go inside and ask to speak with the store manager. If you are able to meet with the manager, look him or her in the eye, extend your hand for a hand-shake, introduce yourself, and express your interest in the job. Most managers are impressed by friendly, outgoing people who are unafraid to initiate a conversation. Tell the manager what a willing worker you are and why you feel this position will be perfect for you. You may still be asked to complete an application, but this impromptu interview may give you a leg up on the competition and may help you stand out in the employer's mind.

Employer Wish List

Here's a type of "employer wish list." Study it well and try to determine which traits you have and which traits you need to work on. Again, be honest with yourself, because if you answer dishonestly, you're only hurting yourself. You don't have to memorize the list, just work on it as you continue your search for the right job for you.

You never know when you'll stumble upon a "Now Hiring" sign, but it's safe to assume that if the sign is still in the window, the position is still open.

Employers want you to…

1. *Be well-groomed.* This is listed first because first impressions are extremely important. Remember, no matter what the current clothing trends happen to be, neatness counts.

2. *Have good oral and written communication skills.* You don't have to be the best speaker in the world, or the greatest writer, but if you can express yourself well and in a pleasant manner, you'll go a long way.

3. *Be reliable.* Employers must know they can depend on you to come to work and do what you're supposed to do.

4. *Be punctual.* Coming to work is great, but if you come late, you may mess up everyone else's schedule.

5. *Be someone who can be trusted*, no matter what position you're in, but most especially if you handle money or confidential information.

6. *Be courteous and nonthreatening.* Your employer or supervisor may need to give lots of orders to keep the business running smoothly, and these orders may not always be pleasant. But whether they are pleasant or not, employers need to know they can give these orders without wondering whether you'll be offended or take them the wrong way.

7. *Be positive and have a "can-do" attitude.* This will uplift everyone's spirits and make it seem as if anything is possible.

8. *Be willing to learn.* Not all jobs are as easy as they seem, so employers want to know that you will accept suggestions and constructive criticism, and you will not be resistant to instruction.

9. *Be self-motivated.* Employers want to know that your supervisor won't have to "light a fire under you" to get you to do something.

10. *Be ambitious.* Employers love enthusiasm, especially when it helps to further their own businesses. An ambitious employee can be of great benefit to company.

Hopefully, with these job-hunting resources at your fingertips and the employer wish list as your guide, it won't take long to find a job. But just in case you find yourself submitting dozens of applications, here's another tip: be sure to make copies of every application you submit. Most black-and-white copies are reasonably priced at places like Staples, Office Depot, or FedEx. This way, you'll remember where you've applied and how you answered each question in case you get a callback and an employer wants to question you further.

CHAPTER FOUR

Getting a Callback

This is it. After days, weeks, or longer of nonstop job hunting, you finally get that call. An employer has looked over your application, résumé, and cover letter and is interested in an interview. You can relax now, right? Wrong. Getting a callback and preparing for the interview requires almost as much work as the initial job hunt.

When you first submitted your application, you probably knew only one thing about the company: It was hiring. But now it's time to do your homework and learn all you can about the company and the person you might be working for. You'll do this by first reviewing the application you submitted (you were advised to keep copies of your applications in the previous section) to refresh your memory on how you answered each question.

To get more details about the company, talk with a friend or relative who perhaps patronizes the company often and ask what he or she loves about the place or which night is the busiest. If you don't know anyone who patronizes the company, you can make a few anonymous phone calls to the office and find out for yourself. For example, if you're interviewing at a restaurant, you may call and ask which menu (breakfast, lunch, or dinner) is the most requested or what the restaurant is known for. This way, in the interview, you can say

Getting a callback for the very first time is a wonderful feeling. Now learn all you can about the business and the person you'll be working for.

something like, "I've heard about your delicious hot wings all over town, and I can't wait to learn how to make them." Another way to do your homework is to visit your library's local history department, which usually keeps newspaper clippings on various businesses in your area. Browse through these files for information about the company, its managers, and any special activities the company engages in, like sponsoring school sports teams or offering scholarships to deserving children. You can also look at the restaurant's Web site or Yelp reviews online.

The application you completed may not have included a job description, so if you want to know more about the potential duties of the job, run a Google or Yahoo! search for a detailed description. Your search will bring up companies across the United States that are hiring for the same position, so be sure to read these descriptions carefully to get a feel for the wide range of tasks someone in this position might be asked to perform. Then, when it's your turn to ask questions during the interview, you can say something like, "I know that prep cooks prepare the kitchen for the actual chef, but I read somewhere that they also do some light cooking. Is that true?"

To prepare for the interview, do a little role-playing. Have a friend or relative assume the role of the employer and ask you questions that the employer might ask. Afterward, have your friend or relative tell you which answers seemed strong, and which need a little work. If no one is available to play the part of the employer, practice answering the questions aloud in front of a mirror. This way, you can watch your own facial expressions to see whether you seem tense or nervous when answering certain questions. These practice sessions will help the actual interview feel less scary and unfamiliar.

Practice makes perfect—especially practice in front of a mirror. Use the mirror to check your posture, your smile, and your facial expression and body language as you answer interview questions.

Interview Practice Questions

Following is a list of sample questions you may be asked during your interview. If you have a friend or relative who works in the same type of position you're applying for, ask the person to describe what he or she remembers about the first interview and the types of questions that were asked. Find out which questions were stumbled over or what was done to prepare for the interview. Make notes so that you can benefit from that person's experience. Feel free to add any other questions you think the employer might ask.

a) Tell me all about yourself.

b) What were your grades in school?

c) What interests you about this job?

d) Why do you feel you're the best person for this job?

e) What do you know about our company?

f) Tell me about your job experience.

g) What experience do you have _____?

(For example, "cleaning a grill," "washing a stack of dishes," "mopping a floor.")

h) What are your strengths? Weaknesses?

(For example, can you stand on your feet for hours at a time? Do you learn fast? These are strengths. Do you live far away and need to make a long commute to work? This is a weakness.)

i) What salary are you looking for?

j) How does this position fit in with your career path?

(Say something like, "This fits into my plans because I eventually want to become a private chef, and this gives me the start I need.")

k) What questions do you have for me?

HOW CAN I OWN MY OWN FOOD TRUCK?

Do you dream of owning your own food truck? If you love cooking and don't want to be tied to one spot, a mobile food business may be the way to go. Go to city hall before you spend any money and find out the laws, codes, and permits you'll need. If you still want your own food truck, think about buying used. New trucks are expensive, so many people remodel used trucks or even trailers and make them into the mobile kitchens of their dreams. Just make sure that if you do buy used, the title is clear, you have a valid driver's license, and your new business-on-wheels can pass emissions. Once all this is done, you can think about what you want to sell and whom you want to sell it to (breakfast or lunch crowd, children, tourists, etc.). Also, make sure you're ready for everything, including breakdowns, bad weather, flash crowds, and grumpy customers.

As you practice, don't just think about acing the interview; also think about what you will do after it ends. You don't want to lose touch with the employer, so you must figure out how to keep the line of communication open between the two of you. For example, as the interview comes to an end, ask how soon the employer expects to make a decision and whether it's OK to call for updates from time to time. If he says it's OK, ask which days and times are best for him to receive your call. Ask if he has a business card, and offer him yours, if you have one. These days, it's easy to get great-looking, inexpensive business cards. Look online for good deals on quality business cards.

Make sure you look your best for the interview by taking your time with your makeup and wardrobe. When you're finished, get a parent or friend's opinion to be sure you're on the right track.

Next, think about how you'll dress for the interview. It's a must that you dress appropriately because this will be the employer's first impression of you.

Women: Your hair should be neat, clean, and well-combed, and your makeup should be tasteful and not too bright. Tattoos should be covered, especially if they are spread over large areas like your arms, chest, or legs. Piercings, if you have them, should be taken out of your nose, lips, eyebrows, and cheeks. Dresses should not be too short or tight, and if you wear a blouse, it should not show too much cleavage or bare skin on the chest or back. In other words, spaghetti-strapped blouses, miniskirts, and "club wear" are out. Also, choose your shoes wisely because the employer might take you on a walking tour of the building, and shoes with extremely high heels may be very uncomfortable.

Men: Your hair should be clean and neatly trimmed. Your pants should be clean and neatly pressed, and they should fit well. This means no drooping or sagging pants, and definitely no underwear peeking out, even if it is a name brand. Depending upon the type of position you're interviewing for, you don't necessarily need to wear a suit. Casual wear, like a nice white shirt and dark pants with a belt should do just fine. Tame long hair, cover all tattoos, go easy on the jewelry, and take out all piercings in order to give the best impression.

The Interview

At long last, it's time for your face-to-face interview. You know the date and time of the interview and the job you'll be trying for. All you need now is to go through your mental checklist before you head out the door.

First, lay out what you plan to wear the night before, then get a good night's sleep so you'll be fresh and alert for the interview the next morning. When you wake, have a good breakfast because breakfast helps you concentrate and also ensures that your brain is at its most alert. Next, double-check your wardrobe to make sure your clothes are clean and wrinkle-free and that they cover up any tattoos or piercings before you leave. While you're at it, double-check your "interview package," too. Your interview package consists of all the things you should take with you to help the interview go smoothly. Here's a quick checklist:

1. Your Social Security card
2. Your driver's license (or state ID)
3. Your business cards, if available
4. A notepad with plenty of clean sheets for making notes
5. An ink pen
6. Your list of personal references (if you didn't include them on your résumé)
7. Extra copies of your résumé

Take time to eat a good, filling breakfast on the morning of your interview so that you can remain clear and focused. Hunger can lead to distraction.

You should have listed some questions for the employer on the notepad because almost every interview ends with the employer asking, "Do you have any questions for me?" Don't be shy about asking questions.

Try to arrive five to ten minutes early so that you have time to take a deep breath, calm your nerves, and mentally prepare for the interview. When you check in with the receptionist, be sure to flash a big smile and be extra polite. The receptionist is part of the very workforce you're trying to join, and the people who do the hiring usually know him or her well.

When you meet your interviewer, offer him or her a handshake. Shake his or her hand just firmly enough to exude confidence. Make sure you say something like, "Hello Mr. Jones, it's great to finally meet you. My name is Larry Smith." Also, wait for the interviewer to lead you to a chair, and don't sit down until he or she instructs you.

You've prepared well for your interview, so when it begins, try to relax and enjoy it. Whatever you do, keep smiling and remember to be yourself.

Facial expressions and body language are both important, so when the two of you sit to begin the interview, lean slightly forward in your chair as if you're really interested in the conversation. Make eye contact. Pay close attention to whatever the interviewer is saying, take notes if necessary, and whatever you do, don't yawn while he or she is speaking. When you talk about yourself or answer questions, be sure your tone of voice remains pleasant. If the employer makes comments that make you uncomfortable, like saying you don't have enough experience, don't get defensive. Employers want to know they're hiring

YOUR SOCIAL NETWORKING PAGES MAY AFFECT YOUR EMPLOYMENT

Did you know that more and more employers check Facebook, Twitter, LinkedIn, and other social networking pages when they are considering someone for employment? It's true. These pages give employers important clues about what type of person you are, but they also tell the employer what type of people you associate with. You don't have to delete your networking pages, and you certainly don't have to begin deleting friends. However, you should be aware that the content on your pages may play a big role in how the employer sees you and whether you will be hired. Look closely at the content on your page. If you don't feel it reaches a certain standard of professionalism, you may consider hiding or deleting certain items.

a pleasant person who is easygoing and gets along well with others.

Last but not least, remember the importance of a good attitude. It's very possible that you won't know the answer to every question you're asked, and some questions may catch you off guard and make it seem as though the employer is trying to make things hard for you. Stay calm and answer to the best of your ability. Anger won't get you a job; it will just get you a short interview and a quick escort out the door. Remember, being steady, pleasant, and easygoing throughout the interview will take you a long way.

CHAPTER SIX

Keeping Your New Job: Standing Out Among the Competition

Snagging a job is a wonderful thing, but holding on to it is even better. These days, with competition as fierce as it is, you may have to contend with other teens, young adults, middle-aged workers, and even senior citizens trying to steal your job away from you. For this reason, you truly must have the proper skills and work ethic if you expect to hold on to your job.

First, be punctual. Not only do employers expect you to show up every day that you're on the work schedule, they also expect you to be on time. In fact, showing up five or ten minutes earlier than your scheduled time is even better. Why? Because your employer will know he or she can depend on you. If you're late, your employer will worry about whether you'll be able to make it in at all, and instead of concentrating on what needs to be done that day, he or she will be focused on whether other workers need to be rounded up to take your place.

Keeping a job can be just as challenging as snagging it. Build your reputation by arriving a few minutes early, wearing a smile, and making your best effort to do what is asked of you.

Attendance is just as important as punctuality. Employers hate it when employees call in sick unexpectedly because someone still has to do the work. This means the employer must round up employees who may be enjoying a day off or must simply pile your work on whoever shows up that day. Even worse, if there's no one available to take your load, the employer may have to fill in for you. This definitely won't put your employer in a good mood.

Next, make sure you dress appropriately for your new job. You snagged the job by dressing like a professional during the interview, and your employer won't expect any less once you begin showing up on a daily basis. Even if you're a dishwasher, table busser, or server, you still need to dress appropriately. This means no plunging necklines, no see-through blouses, no open shirts that show your chest, no tattoos, no sagging pants, and no words or symbols carved into your haircut.

As you become acquainted with your job and the responsibilities that go along with it, be sure to pay close attention to details, because details can make all the difference in the world. Listen closely to everything your supervisor or mentor tells you. In fact, make a habit of repeating what has been said, just to double-check your understanding.

Of course, your workday won't be all work. You will have ample opportunity to interact with

Enjoy your breaks at the company water cooler or break area, but keep the conversation light, keep your personal information to yourself, and don't comment on gossip.

your coworkers, so make sure you're always at your friend-liest. Smile, say good morning to your colleagues, respond pleasantly when your employer or mentor asks something of you, and try your best to always get along with others. This makes for a pleasant workplace and may actually reduce the stress that goes along with dealing with multiple types of personalities. It will also make you stand out as friendly and easy to get along with.

Whatever you do, make sure you practice proper "water cooler" etiquette. The water cooler is that place in the work world where employees commonly gather for a cup of water but end up gossiping about every subject imaginable. Of course, there may not be a water cooler in your building; there may simply be a break room or outside area where everyone gathers. Whatever the scenario, you should still be

IS A PROMOTION IN YOUR FUTURE?

Whatever position you take, set your goal for the way you would like your career to unfold. Ask your employer what it takes to move to the next level. For example, if you're a chef's assistant, find out what you must do to become a chef, then work on that area. Find out if it's possible to volunteer some time on your days off or afternoons so that you can learn under a willing mentor. This volunteer time doesn't need to be done at the place you work; you can volunteer at other restaurants so that you learn a variety of skills.

careful about controlling your conversation. Telling people you barely know your personal business or listening to all of theirs can be dangerous.

Remember, your employer expects you to be professional, so act this way. That is not to say that you can't have fun, it just means that most employers feel you represent their company. By all means, act responsibly. There may be dire consequences if you don't.

These tips and reminders may seem a bit overwhelming at times, but don't let this bother you. Learning to work side-by-side with colleagues and customers is an art that takes practice and patience. To master this art, you just need to be friendly, follow instructions, learn your job inside and out, and do what is expected of you.

The rest will come in time.

bussing Cleaning off or setting a table, including wiping away food particles, replacing dishes and silverware, and carrying dirty dishes to the sink to be washed.

cargo bay A loading dock that attaches to a building where delivery vehicles can pull up close and unload their content and employees can receive the content and take it inside the store.

condiments Anything edible, such as carrots, tomatoes, olives, onions, or even sauces, that can be added to a menu to enhance the food served.

dropped In this instance, it means to lower food into cooking oil or a fryer.

entry-level Describes a job that is obtainable by a person who has limited or no experience. Usually includes on-the-job training.

etiquette Practicing a certain code of behavior.

executive The top person in that field who has the authority to put plans and rules into effect.

gourmet food Any food with high-quality ingredients that are typically thought to be cooked for and consumed by the wealthy.

impromptu Done without having been planned, usually on the spur of the moment.

mentor A trusted instructor, counselor, or teacher who passes information and technique to a learner.

minimum wage The lowest wage that must be paid to an employee for performing a service. Minimum wage is fixed by law and may vary from year to year, company to company, or country to country.

OJT On-the-job training.

personality Personal qualities (like cheerfulness, humor, or intelligence) that make an individual unique and interesting.

pound the pavement To walk the streets looking for a job until one is found.

prep To prepare.

sample A small part or amount of something that shows customers what the entire thing would taste like. For example, to increase sales, a bakery may have to offer sample slices of their cakes and pies.

shadow To follow someone (like a shadow) for a few hours or all day long in order to understand what a particular job entails.

shift manager A person who supervises other people who work a specified shift, like nine to five.

special driver's license A driver's license with an endorsement that allows the driver to transport special people or products.

specialty foods Foods that are original, have special or rare ingredients, are packaged differently, or require a different method of processing than that of "regular" food. Examples: caviar, truffles, gluten-free fudge, and/or soy-free chocolate.

stock boy/girl A person responsible for storing products or keeping store shelves full and organized.

tailoring Tweaking something, such as a résumé, to fit a particular position.

VIP Very important person.

FOR MORE INFORMATION

American Farm Bureau Federation
600 Maryland Avenue SW
Suite 1000W
Washington, DC 20024
(202) 406-3600
Web site: http://www.fb.org
This is an independent, nongovernmental, voluntary organi-
zation governed by and representing farm and ranch
families united to achieve educational improvement,
economic opportunity, and social advancements, and
promote the national well-being.

Canadian Restaurant and Foodservices Association
316 Bloor Street West
Toronto, ON M5S 1W5
Canada
(800) 387-5649
Web site: http://www.crfa.ca
This association represents every sector of Canada's food
service industry, including restaurants, bars, cafeterias, coffee
shops, and contract and social caterers.

ConAgra, Inc.
One ConAgra Drive
Omaha, NE 68102-5001
(402) 595-4000
Web site: http://www.conagra.com
ConAgra is one of North America's largest packaged foods
companies.

Food & Consumer Products of Canada
100 Sheppard Avenue East, Suite 600

Toronto, ON M2N 6N5
Canada
(416) 510-8024
Web site: http://www.fcpc.ca
This is Canada's largest industry association representing
   companies that manufacture and distribute the vast
   majority of food, beverages, and consumer goods on
   grocery store shelves.

Food Info Net, Inc.
P.O. Box 142115
Coral Gables, FL 33114-2115
(305) 613-0123
Web site: http://www.foodinfonet.com
This Internet portal is devoted exclusively to the global
   food industry.

Kraft Foods, Inc.
800 Westchester Avenue
Rye Brook, NY 10573-1301
(914) 335-2500
Web site: http://www.kraftfoods.com
This food and beverage conglomerate manufactures many
   foods, including beverages, cheeses, dairy foods, snack
   foods, confectionary foods, and convenience foods.

McDonald's
One McDonald's Plaza
Oak Brook, IL 60523
(630) 623-3000
Web site: http://www.mcdonalds.com
McDonald's is currently the world's largest chain of hamburger

fast-food restaurants and one of the most popular places for teens to work.

National Association for the Specialty Food Trade, Inc.
136 Madison Avenue, 12th Floor
New York, NY 10016
(212) 482-6440
Web site: http://www.SpecialtyFood.com
This is a not-for-profit business trade association established in 1952 to foster trade, commerce, and interest in the specialty food industry.

United Food and Commercial Workers International Union (UFCW)
1775 K Street NW
Washington, DC 20006
(202) 223-3111
Web site: http://www.ufcw.org
The UFCW is the union that represents workers primarily in the food industry.

Web Sites

Due to the changing nature of Internet links, Rosen Publishing has developed an online list of Web sites related to the subject of this book. This site is updated regularly. Please use this link to access the list:

http://www.rosenlinks.com/JOBS/Food

Aubrey, Sarah Beth. *The Profitable Hobby Farm: How to Build a Sustainable Local Foods Business.* Hoboken, NJ: Howell Book House, 2010.

Aubrey, Sarah Beth. *Starting & Running Your Own Small Farm Business.* North Adams, MA: Storey Publishing, LLC, 2008.

Boulud, Daniel. *Letters to a Young Chef: Art of Mentoring.* New York, NY: Basic Books, 2006.

Carle, Megan. *Teens Cook Dessert.* Berkeley, CA: Ten Speed Press, 2006.

Chamberlain Bros. *In My Mother's Kitchen: 25 Writers on Love, Cooking and Family.* New York, NY: Penguin Group, 2006.

The Culinary Institute of America. *Remarkable Service: A Guide to Winning and Keeping Customers for Servers, Managers, and Restaurant Owners.* Hoboken, NJ: Wiley, 2009.

Dahmer, Sondra J. *Restaurant Service Basics.* Hoboken, NJ: Wiley, 2008.

Edge, John T. *The Truck Food Cookbook: 150 Recipes and Ramblings from America's Best Restaurants on Wheels.* New York, NY: Workman Publishing Company, 2012.

Ferguson, Sheila. *Careers in Focus: Food.* New York, NY: Ferguson Publishing, 2007.

Gold, Rosanne. *Eat Fresh Food: Awesome Recipes for Teen Chefs.* New York, NY: Bloomsbury USA, 2009.

Largen, Velda L. *Guide to Good Food.* Tinley Park, IL: Goodheart-Willcox Co., 2008.

Littrell, J. J., James H. Lorenz., and Harry T. Smith. *From School to Work.* Tinley Park, IL: Goodheart-Willcox Co, 2008.

Mintzer, Rich. *Start Your Own Food Truck Business.* Irvine, CA: Entrepreneur Press, 2011.

Perlich, Martin. *The Art of the Interview.* Los Angeles, CA: Silman-James Press, 2007.

Philips, Alan. *The Complete Idiot's Guide to Starting a Food Truck Business.* New York, NY: Alpha, 2012.

Plunket, Jack W. *Plunkett's Food Industry Almanac 2010: Food Industry Market Research, Statistics, Trends & Leading Companies.* Houston, TX: Plunkett Research, Ltd., 2010.

Schultze, Quentin J. *Résumé 101: A Student and Recent-Grad Guide to Crafting Résumés and Cover Letters That Land Jobs.* Berkeley, CA: Ten Speed Press, 2012.

Spencer, Tricia. *Tips, the Server's Guide to Bringing Home the Bacon.* Mira Loma, CA: Lilac Bloom Press, 2006.

Waldman, Joshua. *Job Searching with Social Media for Dummies.* Hoboken, NJ: Wiley, 2011.

Weber, David. *The Food Truck Handbook: Start, Grow, and Succeed in the Mobile Food Business.* Hoboken, NJ: Wiley, 2012.

BIBLIOGRAPHY

Chalmers, Irena. *Food Jobs: 150 Great Jobs for Culinary Food Lovers.* New York, NY: Beaufort Books, 2008.

Christen, Carol, and Richard N. Bolles. *What Color Is Your Parachute? For Teens, 2nd Edition: Discovering Yourself, Defining Your Future.* New York, NY: Crown Publishing, 2010.

Creators of Top Chef. *How to Cook Like a Top Chef.* San Francisco, CA: Chronicle Books LLC, 2010.

Devantier, Alecia T., and Carol A. Turkington. *Extraordinary Jobs in the Food Industry.* New York, NY: Ferguson Publishing, 2006.

Hall, Stephen. *Sell Your Specialty Food: Market, Distribute, and Profit from Your Kitchen Creation.* New York, NY: Kaplan Publishing, 2008.

Hill, Kathleen. *Career Opportunities in the Food and Beverage Industry.* New York, NY: Facts On File, 2010.

McAlpine, Margaret. *Working in the Food Industry.* New York, NY: Gareth Stevens, 2005.

Mendelsohn, Spike. *The Good Stuff Cookbook: Burgers, Fries, Shakes, Wedges, and More.* Hoboken, NJ: John Wiley & Sons, Inc., 2010.

Schultze, Quentin J. *Resume 101: A Student and Recent-Grad Guide to Crafting Resumes and Cover Letters That Land Jobs.* New York, NY: Crown Publishing, 2012.

Smilow, Rick, and Anne E. McBride. *Culinary Careers: How to Get Your Dream Job in Food (With Advice from Top Culinary Professionals).* New York, NY: Clarkson Potter Publishers, 2010.

About the Author

Rita Lorraine Hubbard was a special educator for more than twenty years. She writes full-time, reviews for the *New York Journal of Books,* and is the author of *African Americans of Chattanooga: A History of Unsung Heroes.* She also manages several Web sites for aspiring writers.

Photo Credits

Cover, p. 1 © iStockphoto.com/ariwasabi; cover (background), back cover, p. 3, interior page background image © iStockphoto.com/gerenme; p. 5 Kathleen Finlay/Radius Images/Getty Images; pp. 8–9 AFP/Getty Images; pp. 12–13, 17 Bloomberg/Getty Images; pp. 14–15 © iStockphoto.com/CandyBox Images; pp. 18–19, 41 © AP Images; pp. 22–23 Robert Nickelsberg/Getty Images; p. 25 Creatas/Thinkstock; pp. 28–29 Boston Globe/Getty Images; p. 30 Scott Olson/Getty Images; pp. 32–33 Stockbyte/Thinkstock; p. 35 © iStockphoto.com/Diane Diederich; pp. 38, 60–61 iStockphoto/Thinkstock; pp. 42–43 Andrew Burton/Getty Images; pp. 46–47 Spencer Platt/Getty Images; p. 51 Roberto Westbrook/Blend Images/Getty Images; p. 53 Jamie Grill/The Image Bank/Getty Images; p. 56 Rob Melnychuk/Brand X Pictures/Getty Images; p. 59 Sean Malyon/Photolibrary/Getty Images; p. 65 Ingram Publishing/Thinkstock; pp. 66–67 Jupiterimages/Brand X Pictures/Getty Images.

Designer: Nicole Russo; Editor: Bethany Bryan;
Photo Researcher: Amy Feinberg